Mirage

Mother's Best Kept Secrets

L.Yingling

ISBN-10: 1724342916

ISBN-13: 978-1724342911

First Printing Edition 2018.

L. Yingling

P.O. Box 183

Quinton, VA, 23141

https://clichecoutureshop.com/featured

*Mirage Mother's Best Kept Secrets * L. Yingling

Contents

The Re-Occurring Illusion of Death:

Have you ever considered what it's like to experience a reoccurring illusion of death? Your flawed senses deceive you because your environment has become so miserable. Imagine dying, or lying in agony, night after night, drenched in sweat, waiting for it to pass. They could hear your blood-curdling screams from miles away, if not for being silenced, by fear. It appears as though your pulse couldn't fade anymore before it stops altogether. Only by being broken down, in such a way, could you understand. The abuse numbs your body, but your soul still suffers from each blow. It's an endless film stuck on replay, the slowest, surest death, that happens, over and over, with no promise of stopping. Each day you awake, wondering if it will be your last.

You wished to avoid an uproar, but the sound of breaking dishes tells you: it's too late. He is furious, and his anger knows no limits. The fire in his powerful brown eyes says you are lucky to be alive, but inside you've already perished. Though you're a fearless woman, you have met your match.

He persuaded that he was the perfect gentleman and swept you off your feet. Somehow, you fell right into his trap. Those fearful eyes were once the same ones you gazed into, and all your problems became distant. The butterflies you felt were

L. Yingling

those of the most delicate, unexplainable feelings, known to human. A young stage of a flourishing love, told in the most magical fairytales, ever read. How does the same guy, sent to rescue you, become your most feared enemy? You have spent hours talking, laughing, and sharing your deepest secrets with one another. There was nothing the two of you couldn't accomplish together. Just as your youthful dreams become your existence, somehow they shift into your worst nightmares. By the time you realize, you've been sucked into his narcissistic realm, with no escape in sight, it's too late and passed the point of no return. Nobody can spare you. They will only judge your stupidity for remaining with him.

After trying to escape, he reels you back in without fail, every time. Not only are you weakened by fear, but he stalks you, so much that you see him while you're sleeping. You take an alternate route to work every day, hoping he won't follow, yet in a glance up at your mirror, you see his face, in that of a stranger's. He shows up at the most unusual places with an expression that reads "You'll never be able to escape me" You're convinced the kids will suffer tremendously if you end the relationship. You try so hard to avoid exposing them to the monster their dad really is, but he continues to reveal himself. At bedtime, you hear them cry, "I want my daddy" since regardless, they still love and adore him, despite the monster he's become. You dig deep, but cannot find the words to comfort them because you too have become a monster, consumed by hate.

Your poor judgment blinds you from seeing how the fighting only denies them of their bliss, and robs their innocence, causing them to react. Now, you are left to deal with their abnormal behavior, as well as the ordinary battle for your life. You watch the lifetime movies, where others end up dead, yet still, clutch the idea that someday he might change. Eventually, they will question whether or not, you have been brainwashed. The loud voices in your head, screaming "GET OUT" offer no suggestion as to how you should do so. The confusion eventually gets quieter and becomes normal, leaving you defenseless to his capacity.

Hannah's story may not be yours, but if you have such illusions, you can relate in a way that no other will comprehend, unless having experienced it for themselves. Hannah reflects back to her childhood and so desperately wonders how she wound up here.

1 Reflection of A Child

It was just announced over the loudspeaker "GUEST SPEAKERS ARE HERE; EVERYONE REPORT TO THE AUDITORIUM" My immediate thoughts were "this is just going to be another long, boring speech everyone couldn't care less about" When strolling down the hall, it was clear we all had similar thoughts. Entering the auditorium as a child resembles entering a football stadium as a grown-up. It was colossal. As we took our seats, the only noise anyone could hear was prattling voices of the entire Fourth-Grade class, loud and unclear. The lights dimmed, and the conversations had calmed. The guest speaker moves toward the microphone and patiently waits for the chitchat to silence. She starts by introducing herself "Hello Students, thank you for having me here today" then she proceeds onward to discussing different colleges, the long-term benefits, and how we should prepare now, while in the early years of our school career. They penetrated this idea in our heads, from one speech to another. One day, in Language class, the teacher gave us a task to write our future objectives; at last, it clicked. Despite my parent's financial status, this would be my "way out" of the poverty I had become so familiar with.

 From that day on, I'd stare off into space, daydreaming of college, making my mom and dad proud, and becoming successful. Envisioning myself in another state, Florida, beyond any doubt, sounded great! Where it's warm and radiant throughout most of the year, palm trees cover the campus grounds and I'd finally be so far away from here. I became so fond of the idea and eventually mentioned it to my parents. As we sat at the dinner table to eat, I blurted out. "Mom and Dad I want to go to college after I graduate" For a moment, they stopped chewing their food, then smiled and changed the subject. Boy! What a slap in the face. They brushed it off, without a mere word of encouragement. Humiliation quickly replaces my excitement. Instead of giving up, I remained quiet about the idea. I get, it's less demanding to change the subject, instead of clarifying how costly it may be, or how hard I'd need to work to guarantee my acceptance. Perhaps they figured I wouldn't understand.

   Hannah knew her parents didn't have much money, and probably wouldn't take her serious, but she did not arrange being ignored. Neither, was she prepared for feeling unworthy of having enormous dreams. She sought after, no less than, an honest expression of encouragement. Instead, Hannah felt as though her ideas were absurd and implausible.

2 Pre-determined Destiny

April 14, 2006; Good Friday and we are out of school, for Spring Break. The grand plans of going to the mud bog with daddy went out the window. I looked forward to seeing the big trucks get stuck in the mud holes and hearing the boisterous motors thunder, instead; I am being punished. I guess it's fairly ordinary, nowadays. I fell asleep in Social Studies class again, and my teacher called home. This is the most tormenting class ever. The teacher is nice, I suppose, but his long addresses of History, seem so insignificant and put me fast to sleep. In fact, the only time I do not sleep in his class is when we have group activities. Other times, we are lucky when he displays visuals, to go with his dreadful lessons. It wasn't until I returned home to realize; he called my parents. I can still hear my dad saying, "If you don't do well in school, you will quit your job". McDonald's is not the greatest job, but a good start. In the past, I was more engaged and doing well in school, receiving awards and basketball trophies, which made me proud. As I grew older, I wanted something more, other than education. I wanted to buy a nice pair of brand name shoes. Clothes of my choice would be nice. Feeling accepted and commendable enough to hang out with the cool kids at school, was an agenda. They have wealthy parents and don't want or need for much.

  Somewhere along the way, I had become rebellious. On the day of the Mud Bog, I told mom, my car needs an oil change. I took full advantage of the opportunity, and detoured along the way. With the windows rolled down, booming my new CD, I sing every word loud and proud, confident I sounded just like Mariah Carey. After making a few stops, I met up with friends, and we go out for lunch. It's true what they say, time flies when you're having fun. A couple hours quickly turns into four, then five, though it didn't matter, while I was having fun and laughing, without a care in the world. After returning home, I find out that besides being punished, I too had to hand over the keys to my car since it took longer than expected. It seems I am handing them over more and more, these days.

  Hannah was all but compliant. Rather than owning her faults, she removes her things from the car, and while handing the keys to her dad, she tells him "you can keep the car" Hannah becomes incensed, and grows tired of persistently having the car she worked so hard for, taken away. She ponders back and forth, thinking about what happened that day and the days prior. As they always do, her immature feelings gradually take their course. With an unwillingness to recognize that it was merely her poor choices influencing the restrictions, it only provokes her, all the more. Hannah becomes so frustrated that her next decision, could ultimately change her destiny.

My thoughts race, from one feeling to the next. "I'm tired of this, I can't and won't do it any longer" I made a phone call to a close friend, with a plan to run away. She thinks I'm crazy, but nevertheless, agrees to pick me up. I put together the perfect plan. With no one noticing, I need to pack my stuff and put it somewhere I could easily grab when my ride shows up. Daddy will be gone all day, and mama is sleeping. While waiting anxiously, I fear she will wake before I leave and my plans would be ruined. I was unsure of how things would turn out, and neither didn't care much. There was, but one thing I was sure of, I required more for my life, than what was being advertised.

The time moves so slow and it's getting dark when my friend pulls up. Once I get in the car, and we drive away, it was a relief, but my thoughts are still all over the place. The intense throbbing of my heartbeat is a sure sign I am in for a thrill. Although I show no hint of regret, she asks me several times "Are you sure". With a nod, I pretend to be more than confident. The dark back roads seem to stretch for hundreds of miles and we may never make it far enough away from home, that I can comfortably say, I made my escape, without getting caught. What normally takes 15 minutes to get to the nearest gas station, feels like hours.

We roll the windows down, our hair blowing in the warm spring breeze, while the music is booming. The only things seen are the headlights in front and the few deer we encounter. First stop is the gas station, where we pull in with our favorite song blaring, portraying ourselves to be wild and free, as we always do.

3 Free at last; Stuck at best

Staying with friends, sleeping on different couches night after night, with no money, I often wonder where my next meal might come from. The growling of my stomach is a reminder that if nothing else, I must eat. Some nights I get lucky and my friend, who works at Applebee's shows up with leftover food. I devour each bite as if it were the most anticipated feast on Thanksgiving. Before today, my Mom's melt in your mouth Ham, that she would spend hours cooking on only two occasions out of the year, was the best. As for now, there is absolutely nothing that tastes as good as the dry, long set out, Chicken wings from Applebee's.

  The thought of my parents finding me is frightening, but I must get a job. I walk to the nearby Mall every day where it's always crowded, asking for applications. There are many families getting pictures taken with the Easter Bunny. Observing a stranger's smiling face and hearing their loud laughter is enough to put me in a lonely place. The Mall never appeared to be so big, in the same way, I have never felt this small. My mind plays tricks on me, with each corner I turn, I imagine my mom and dad there, waiting for me, furious and ready to take me home. The adrenaline of my heart hustling is so loud it muffles the clamor of the busy shoppers. I hustle along, stopping at a few stores on my way out, to ask if they are hiring. "I'M NERVOUS" must be written all over my face. The responses are not very promising, "We won't be hiring again for a few months'" says a few clerks. I spend nearly two weeks going back and forth, filling out dozens of applications. With no luck, I begin doubting myself and eventually, quit trying.

   Meanwhile, I make a few friends, who could get into the eighteen and older clubs. We spend most, every weekend, hopping from one to another. The blaring music that makes it impossible to converse with anybody, drowns out the confusion in my mind. The floor surges of people moving so close that in the event you didn't know how to dance, no one would notice, though we couldn't have cared any less, after two or three drinks. Partying was something to expect, each weekend. I engage in different activities that might land me in jail; going neck to neck, fighting, drinking and driving, and smoking pot, but, I always got lucky. I am now, so far from what I originally set out to do and being successful didn't matter much, anymore.

   Although I can't pinpoint what it is, there is still, an overwhelming feeling of hollowness. Every burning shot of Vodka and the frequent late nights with the crowd make it easy to ignore. We have become frequent flyers at the Waffle House, on the weekends. The smell of hash browns cooking at two in the morning is a sign, we will sober up soon, then pass out, only to do it over again the next night. The fun had to end at some point, as it always does. I assume everyone got bored, doing the same things, seeing the same faces, at the same clubs, every weekend. Reality sets back in and takes the place of friends, who become far and few.

Hannah previously experimented with Marijuana, but was now exposed to Hard Core street drugs. The once before, unfamiliar smell of crack being prepared, similar to burning plastic, had become a recognizable fragrance. Witnessing her friends on a cocaine binge for days at a time, giving them a speed high, only to seem so lifeless when coming down, had become an amusement. Watching them share needles as they pump Heroin in their veins; no longer appears to her as unsanitary and disgusting.

In light of Hannah becoming a follower, she could have easily accessed drugs, which didn't look to be so awful; yet something continuously stops her. So-called friends, who make shooting up look fascinating, taunt her. Every line of coke they sniff appears to solve each bit of their problems, but only for a moment's time. I suppose Hannah had an angel, protecting her from that, of the most destructive matters.

It wasn't long before I realize, this present reality, wasn't at all I imagined it to be. "What am I doing? My life is going down the drain" I question everything and start measuring every one of my choices. For a moment, I figured, it may very well be smarter, to go back home than to continue this path, lost and befuddled. I was not getting anywhere. One racing thought after another, imagining how angry my parents must be, I reverted back, to my current problems and convinced myself that going back wasn't a choice. My only option is to find a job and hope that things get better from here. Somewhere along the way, I find enough confidence to give it another shot. Once more, I submit applications, and for the first time in my life, I fall to my knees, crying out in prayer, to a God that I have not, yet been acquainted. I didn't know if I was praying right, but somehow the Sunday school lessons I learned as a child, returned. After realizing that my strong will alone, wouldn't get me where I should be and my luck had run out, I was beyond desperate for any sign of hope.

4 Major Break-through, Disguised

The following day; I wake up feeling a little more positive and dressed more appropriately than the days before, in hopes to make a good impression. Back to the Mall, I go. It was a 5-mile walk, from where I was staying. I didn't have much working knowledge, or a car, and had no money. My alternatives were extremely limited. I must have filled out and submitted an application for every store and restaurant, there.

Much to my surprise, after two days, I receive a call from the Store Manager at ChickFila. He presents himself in a mild-manner, but firm tone and welcomes me for an interview. My confidence skyrocketed, but I contained my energy until we got off the phone. In the days following, I considered what I would wear to the interview and what I should say.

When the big day comes, I am incredibly overwhelmed with anxiety. I shower, put on my best pair of black dress pants with a solid-colored shirt, and douse myself with perfume. As I head to the interview, I notice a hint of Fall drawing near; In the midst of the wind blowing, fell bright colored leaves and the smell of freshly made bread, from the nearby Bakery, fills the air. It was the perfect day for walking, just about anywhere.

As I get closer to the Mall, my thoughts begin to race. Hopefully, he sees past my nervousness and I get the job. I rehearse everything to say once more. It's been a long time coming, and the only interview someone has called me for, I must make it count. With sweaty palms, I enter the food court, planning to cover any sign of anxiety. It must be lunch rush hour because the line of people ordering food is so long, it extends out the door. Finding a quiet place to sit looks impossible. It wasn't long before the store manager comes over and introduces himself. "Mr. Miller, it's a pleasure to meet you" as I shake his hand. When we sit for the interview, I realize, there's nothing to fear. The mild-mannered man I'd spoken to on the phone was similarly as soft-spoken and laid back, face to face. He begins by telling me, "We are not always as busy as we are right now; It just so happens that we've had two busloads of kids on a field trip, come in, so I will make this short" What I relief! I thought. He quickly scans over my application and asks a few general questions. Before I knew it, he is offering me a job on the spot and welcoming me to the Chick Fila Team.

At last, Hannah was to start a job. She couldn't help but wonder, was it an answered prayer? It was the one thing she did differently, this time. She's unsure, but tolerates the thought. Is it possible that a higher power listened to her cry, saw her desperation, and answered the one and only prayer, she had ever submitted? Hannah grasped the idea for a moment, but her uncertainty, directs her away. She makes due, with being lucky. It's likely, her recent behavior, made Hannah think she was uncommendable. Her lack of Faith negated the thought, of being blessed in any way.

I am relieved to start working, but the weather is changing and I am confronted with new issues. Walking five miles to get there isn't so terrible until it rains vigorously or snows and the temperature is below zero. I am fortunate to get a lift on some of those days, but others, I suck it up and walk. I have never loathed the mere sign of rain as much as I do now. It makes for the longest walk ever. A stroll in the park on a sunny day has suddenly turned into what feels like, a cross-country marathon, rain or shine. I have figuratively become the target for the cars speeding along. Whoever splashes the most water from what covers the street has the best aim. The puddles on the sidewalk resemble a maze to avoid. There is no better way to start the workday than with wet socks and shoes. Still, soaking wet, I report to work, to be greeted with stares from Co-workers, wondering why I am drenched. I simply return the greeting, with a smile.

Hannah's smile was not to be mistaken for an effort to make new friends. She did not want, not even so much as to hold a conversation with anybody. She had learned and applied the fake it until you make it, concept. Hannah talks less and spends more time observing. It wasn't long before she assumes that her Co-workers come from different backgrounds than she. With their high dollar shoes, brand new phones, and nice cars; it appears as though their parents are wealthy, and they have much of the things Hannah can only wish she had.

She overhears them whine about their recent dilemmas. "My parents won't buy me the new phone that just came out" or; "They made me get this job to help pay for my stuff" the best one was; "My car is five years old, and my parents won't get me a new one" Their problems are insignificant when contrasted with what she faces. If you were to ask her opinion, someone has spoiled the ungrateful brats, who don't understand just how good they have it.

When Hannah's Co-workers approach her, she engages as little as possible, thinking they have absolutely nothing in common nor, anything to talk about. Hannah realizes later, they too, have their opinions, considering her to be snobby, rather stuck up, but it's more likely that she was just stuck. Hannah avoids revealing her back round at all cost and the possibility of rejection; both of which are more important to her than making friends. Being exempt from the distractions of non-work related, conversations, enables her to learn the job sufficiently. She still struggles with an inconsistent means of transportation to work. It eventually results in her being late on different occasions.

As the rain pours, and my shift will soon start, I am hoping it will ease up. I wait because, my friend guaranteed me a ride, but the rain is just getting heavier, and she has not shown up yet. By the time I get to work, I will be late. My manager, who is a Middle Eastern man and not as calm as the one I interviewed with, pulls me aside and requests a clarification. Similarly, as I had built my confidence when hired, my job will now be in question. I let him know. "It's down-pouring, and I waited for a ride that never came" He reacts firmly, however less cruel than I had expected. "Try not to make it a habit," he says.

Coming from the small county I grew up in, I was a stereotype of this tall, dark-haired, tanned skin, Middle Eastern man, from the first day I worked. I often wonder about his experience; why he came to the United States, how different his way of life must be from what I know, and what the tattoos on his eyelids mean. The only thought I've ever had about the Middle East is that it's a faraway, Third World Country, associated with the people responsible for U.S. terrorist attacks.

Hannah had a solid feeling of curiosity and fear towards her supervisor, although he was calm, and mostly quiet, just as she was. He seems to be sympathetic after she explains, why she was late. This minimized the shame she felt and in the long run, they both would exchange conversation. It was mostly, work-related.

Within two weeks, Hannah was late reporting to work again and like the first occasion, he pulls her to the side; she thought without question, she would lose her job. After giving an explanation and much to Hannah's surprise, he offers her a ride to and from work, each day. She has heard this before by people she considered friends. Hannah couldn't help but think, if her friends would not help, at that point for what reason, would he? Still, she appreciates the kind gesture.

My manager proves me wrong and did exactly what he said he would do. From that day on, he picks me up toward the beginning of the day and drops me back off at night. It was such an alleviation, not worrying about walking a Marathon in the rain or snow. As time advanced, my cliché contemplations of him obscured. We would get to know each other through small talk during the rides to and from work.

5 New Endeavors

After a little while, Hannah's supervisor suggests picking her up to spend personal time together. By now, she was comfortable with him. He didn't appear to be so mysterious any longer. She especially did not want to extend a feeling of ungratefulness, for the favor having been done for her. Hannah was reluctant, at first, yet she eventually agrees. Before she knew it, they both were spending more time together beyond work. They trade stories about where the two originated from and how they ended up in their current circumstances. He explained entering the United States as a Refugee; and how they do not acknowledge him in his country, considering his religion. The terrible tales about what they do to Non-Muslims influences Hannah's reality to appear as though it were of Paradise. "I watched Government Officials torch my neighbor's home, while they were inside," he says. She gave him the quick once over for the most recent occurring events in her life. Developing a bond was inevitable, for them.

In the coming days spent together, he insisted that Hannah did not pay, for anything, not as simple as a meal, or a drink for herself. She wasn't at all, habituated with this kind of treatment, but liked it very much. Often he would check in and ask her if she needed anything. Hannah was happy to have finally found an availing friend.

As you may guess, our friendship quickly evolves into a relationship. I am impressed, and he has practically swept me off my feet. So effortlessly, he charms me with his great sense of humor. He completely shocks me with elegant gifts and takes me to the mall on shopping sprees. His, oh so gentle touch and kind gestures, continue to take my breath away. When I gaze into his big brown eyes, I am confident; we are meant for each other. With every passing day, I end up laughing and smiling a little more. The innocence in his broken English, I have grown to understand and love. We have lengthy discussions about our trusted future with each other. Someplace in the middle, I have perceived his yearning and the hustle he has about him. His Demeanor suggests that he is a speedy mastermind and can arrange pretty much anything he wants. These attributes are good to beat all. It seems, there is no limit to the things we can accomplish with the help of one another. I have fallen head over heels for him.

Hannah was without a doubt, exceptionally inspired, this man shows up, appearing to solve every, last bit of her present issues, gradually acquainting her with a way of life that was much better than what she knew, previously. One day, out of nowhere, he chose he would stop working at Chick-Fila to establish a transportation business. He urges her to quit also and to be his partner. Even though Hannah had no direct experience in maintaining a company, she is amped about the new idea and confident she would learn quickly. With no faltering, Hannah quits her job at Chick Fila and together they explore new Endeavors.

It was difficult, but Hannah is no stranger to taking on new challenges. She assumes, at least now, the hard work may just pay off. It requires them to invest many days on the road at a time, driving and picking up cars from auctions and delivering them to different dealers. After a few months, the long trips and days without rest pay off. They receive more money, in a month's time, than Hannah has ever seen in her life. The more her childhood dreams turn into reality, the more profound her affection for him develops. In so much, that it didn't make a difference what he did, she wouldn't release him, not before putting up a fight, at any rate. She has no clue, the battle she is about to be up against, yet, she will soon find out.

6 Defamation or Deception

I'm so exhausted, but I remind myself day by day that despite the trouble, it'll all be worth it. The days and nights are so long, they begin to run together. I can't distinguish the difference between the two. Evenings are the most challenging because my eyelids get so heavy, and I'm perplexed about dosing off while driving. Though, I suppose it about beats battling the daytime traffic. Our most frequent trips to Maryland, New Jersey, and Washington D.C. are the worst. Almost everyone on the planet takes the bustling Beltway, to get where they have to go, all at once.

It is entertaining to discover the distinctive characteristics of road rage, sitting in traffic, day in and day out. The loud sounding of a horn implies that somebody is in a rush. They think, their offensive gesture will intimidate us and we will move out of their path, as though we have some place else to move to. There is no need, for the cars ahead to turn their radios on since everyone for miles, can hear and feel the loud pounding of the obnoxious neighboring car's music and bass. The motorcyclist, have a favorable position. They can, with little of a stretch, speed past all the traffic, but they would not want a State trooper to catch them doing this.

Learning shortcuts is an absolute requirement. Else, we will never convey our Customers cars within their desired timeframe. I often wonder if any of them travel outside their city limits. They call a few times each day, asking for what reason despite everything we are sitting in rush hour traffic. It's a significant weakness having time constraints and trying to maneuver through traffic in a big truck and trailer, hauling up to five cars behind. I quickly learn that adding vast amounts of weight slows the braking process down tremendously. We pull over and change now and then, but he does most of the driving. With long stretches majority of which we spend talking, our bond just extends. I catch myself glancing over at him all starry-eyed, thinking, this can't be real. Up to this point, my life has progressed so quickly. There is no chance I could turn back. Not even after the run-ins with his purported ex's that insist they are still intimate.

He guarantees me, there is nothing going on and is exceptionally persuasive about it. This one lady whom he dated before me, has become a nuisance. He reassures that she is only grief-stricken by their break-up and will not accept it. Apparently, she has a daughter that looks to him as her father. Sometimes, she uses this to try jolting him back into the relationship. Although I never express it, I have sympathy for the woman and her daughter. I recently notice late-night phone calls he refuses to answer. With a blank stare on his face, I sense he is up to no good. He keeps his phone very near, at all times. Here and there, I notice the insignificant lies, and sometimes he mysteriously disappears, but never without perfect reasoning.

7 Expecting...

Before long, Hannah discovers she is pregnant. Like most women, young, naïve, and vulnerable, she hopes it will change their recent problems, causing them to fight and argue. Through many hot summer days and with little sleep, she continues helping him transport cars; though, after a while, it would take a toll. The further along she gets into the pregnancy, the less she travels with him. Days and time spent apart result in higher suspicions and a significant lack of trust. He continues to reassure her; he is not seeing other women, and that her accusations are all made up in her head. "If you don't stop accusing me of cheating, then I might as well do it, please trust me Hannah" He would say to her. She wants to believe him and somehow he convinces her she was just insecure.

Meanwhile, He continues surprising her with extravagant gifts. The rare jewelry shipped from his country would melt every bit of care away. For her Birthday that year, he buys a Mercedes Benz. Hannah thought back to the little girl, she once was, who assumed that such luxurious cars, were not accessible unless you were of a particular High class. She felt like the luckiest girl in the world. The two of them took a vacation to Texas, and before then, Hannah had been little further away from the small county where she grew up.

All the while, he would still be up to no good. Hannah eventually finds herself on an emotional rollercoaster. She would soon be a first-time mother, with possibly a deceptive partner who she continues to fall in love with. Meanwhile, Hannah tried convincing everyone he was the greatest. Despite his infidelities, he was perfect in her eyes, from the moment he swept her off her feet. Just as she would believe he was faithful, he would eventually mess up again, and she was back on the roller coaster. This was becoming, a vicious cycle that left her more confused.

Hannah spent a lot of her pregnancy with sleepless nights, crying in agony because she could not reach him, sometimes until days later. The mere thought of him being with another woman kills her. He was superb at turning his shortcomings around. He would convince her enough, to where somehow Hannah believes it's her fault and at some point or another, she pushed him away.

In November of that year, Hannah being eight months pregnant had arranged family portraits, which she would frame and give to her mom for Christmas. She had his clothes picked out and just hoped he would not call with an excuse not to come, this had become typical. Hannah doubted him until the minute he arrived. When he did, she was so happy and hopeful. She was like a child who has reunited with her long-lost puppy.

Despite their problems, they still had a connection. Perhaps it was the ambition they both shared, that kept them in-sync, with one another. Maybe it was the young girl in Hannah that held onto hope, believing she had met her soul mate and their dreams may finally come true, together if she would just hold on a little longer. After having pictures done and returning home, she notices pain in her stomach that was not normal. Hannah takes a warm bath, hoping it will pass, but the pain and pressure only get worse. It was as if there was a weight lying on her ribs. After being advised and going to the ER, for what she thought might have been labor pains, turned out to be one of the worst days of her life.

While the doctors hooked her up to several monitors, the two of them would gaze over at each other with confusion and anxiously wait to find out if they would have a baby that night. The doctors couldn't find his heartbeat. At first, Hannah wasn't sure what that meant, though she knew it couldn't be good. The doctors suddenly seem very concerned and the commotion quickly progresses. By the time she realizes, something is wrong; the doctors also realize, her blood count was down to a level two. Between delivering a stillborn baby and being rushed to have an emergency blood transfusion, Hannah's memory of the first couple days in the hospital is blurry.

After recovering from surgery, she wakes up shivering cold, and notices her family surrounded the bed, yet she was still in a daze. "where is my baby, can you bring him to me" she asks. Her eyes close, as she falls back to sleep, for hours. When she finally snaps back, it appears she was still unaware he had passed. Over the next few days, Hannah holds her lifeless baby, every opportunity given. The nurses sadly watch her wrap him in a blanket, to keep from getting cold. She counts his fingers and toes and rocks him in her arms so carefully while humming a song. Hannah stares at him, wondering when he might wake up. His features resemble much of his dad's; slightly tanned skin, thick black hair, and similar eyebrows. Without a mere blemish, Hannah thought of him to be, the most, perfect, healthy, baby. Her smiling down at him shows contentment while watching him sleep in slumber, so peacefully and sound.

She eventually returns home to an empty nursery. Without a baby to care for and seeing all the things they had bought to prepare for his homecoming, it confuses Hannah. She believes it's a bad dream she will eventually wake up from, and her baby would be in her arms, once again. Much to her dismay, it was only wishful hoping, and reality would soon hit like a ton of bricks.

Hannah spends the next few weeks crying for days at a time, grieving the loss alone and feeling empty. Her partner was right back to work before she ever made it home from the hospital. They talk on the phone, and he attempts, but there is nothing, anyone can say, to make her feel better. She needs him there with her now, more than ever before. Her family checks on her, from time to time, but he was the only person who could identify with her misery.

8 Deemed Unstable

At Hannah's follow up appointment the doctor must sense, she is not coping well. He bluntly asked her, "Hannah, are you doing ok?" With no idea, that they would admit her to a psych ward; Hannah explains to him, in so many words, she just wants to be with her baby. The doctor describes the institution as a place where she would find a healthy way to cope with the loss. Hannah quickly finds out, it is not, in fact, the place she needs to be.

When admitted, the staff leads her down a gloomy hallway. She notices there isn't a window in sight; not the slightest peek of sunshine could enter the building. The air lingers of a strong hospital-like smell. As they show her to the room she would stay in, there is no hint of color or decoration that might appeal, not even to the most uncomplicated person. She sighs with grief and regret, while her roommate greets her with a half smile, pointing Hannah to her bed. She remembers the doctor's reassurance, that they will release her, at her own free will, which seems comforting.

During her stay, Hannah is being forced to take medication, she didn't feel she needed. If refused, the staff threatens to put her on the second floor; where she learns, they restrain people, with a straight jacket and confine them to a tiny room made up of patted walls. Afraid, she would finally submit to taking the medication when the staff made their rounds. Hannah fears how long she might last in there.

At bedtime, her roommate could hear her muffled cry. It nearly lasts all night until Hannah eventually falls asleep. Waking in the morning with puffy eyes, her roommate politely asks "How did you end up in here" Hannah sighs, responding with a shrug. "I

---

don't know, but it's only making matters worse" as she thought about being in this place, it seemed to only intensify her grief. Her roommate explains that she will eventually get settled and it won't seem so bad. It was likely impossible for Hannah to grasp the thought of being in there long enough to get comfortable.

 After two days, she had only grown sadder and becomes utterly fed up. Hannah requests a release and learns, it was not as simple as the doctor made it seem. Apparently, the staff determines who may, or may not, be fit for release. This doesn't look very promising, since she had already given them a hard time, refusing the medication. After several desperate attempts of trying to talk her way out, her family visiting and also trying to get her out, the staff finally grant her a determination hearing. Hannah knew this might be her only chance of getting out soon. Although she had never met, the person who would ultimately decide, she tries to imagine what questions he or she might ask. As Hannah lies in bed the night before, she wonders, what would be an inclination that a person, deemed unstable, might get released, and sent home. Hannah knew it was not the right place for her, but that was irrelevant. She had to prove it to a complete stranger.

 The next morning comes, Hannah is prepared to put her grief aside, long enough to make the most favorable impression. During the hearing, she smiles and makes eye contact with the man asking questions. She insists that, other than grieving the loss of her baby, she is mentally stable to return home. Finally, after seven days of what seemed like torture, he approves her release. Hannah's partner did not come to visit, throughout her seven-day stay, but he shows up as she walks out the doors to her freedom, at last. Once again, she is like the child, being reunited, with her long-lost, highly adored, best friend.

If only he knew how his presence makes the worst situations feel bearable, maybe he would try a little harder. My hopeful thoughts gather. I insist on giving him the benefit of the doubt. When we return home, I make a conscious decision that today I must cope and move on. It's not as easy doing, as it is thinking, but I definitely don't want to go back to that place. We spent the next few days packing up our baby's stuff and getting it out of sight. As much as I didn't want to let his things go, I knew this could be a start of the healing process. Meanwhile, we find things to laugh about amid our conversations. We hold each other firmly and cry together. It is in his arms, that I feel most safe and secure, while he stares into my eyes and reassures me we would get through this together.

9 Love or Lust

F all quickly turns into winter, then winter into spring. There is not a day that passes, that Hannah doesn't think of all the things that "could have been, should have been, or would have been"; Lost in thought, she remembers all the nights spent crying and the stress that her partner inflicted, while she was pregnant. She secretly blames him for the death of their son. Her thoughts lead to intense anger of which she had never felt or experienced before then.

While Hannah tries to heal, she can't help, but to think of how her grief started. Not only did she blame her partner for the stress he caused, but she also turns back to God. Only this time, it was in anger. She questions every bit of faith she ever had. "God, if you are real, how could you let this happen" She tries to conceal her anger, especially towards her partner, but it eventually comes out, in an argument.

The secret Hannah tried so hard to cover up, slipped off the tip of her tongue. "You are the reason our son died" For a moment, it becomes so silent that one could distinctly hear a thin sheet of paper hitting the floor. His eyes grew enormous, and his response unravels a violent side she hadn't seen before. He pushes her down and pounds her head against the hardwood floor. Hannah was no stranger to being shocked by his actions, but this was the most shocking thing he had done, yet. She screams, in fear, but that doesn't stop him. "One more pound to the floor would be the last I'd ever recall" it was merely this thought, which gave her enough strength to finally, pull away. She bolts to the bathroom, quickly locks it, and with all of her weight against the door, she sits in anguish.

The shock eventually wears off, and she processes everything that just happened. It must have been hours before Hannah could be sure he had left and it's safe to open the door. Shaking and fumbling for her phone, she immediately calls her closest friend. Perhaps she was ashamed of what had just happened since she only told her friend they had a disagreement, explaining that she needed to get away for a little while.

Within the first few weeks, he makes several attempts a day, but she rejects his calls. He leaves sobbing messages, apologizing for the incident and begging for forgiveness. He promises Hannah, it will never happen again. Meanwhile, staying with her friend isn't ideal and only a temporary alternative. Hannah was back to sleeping on someone's couch, once again. She assumes her friend had not cleaned the cat litter box for days. The smell of urine and feces was stronger than her ability to fall asleep. She would lie there each night, tossing and turning, hoping to get used to the smell. Hannah didn't fall asleep some nights, until the sun rose, in the morning. It made for a long, miserable day.

At some point, Hannah naturally misses him and the home they shared. It's likely she would accept blame for the rage, after thinking they could've avoided the altercation, had she not said those hurtful words. She eventually answers his calls, and on the other end, he cries, begging and pleading for her to return home. His apology seems genuine as he claims it will never happen again. Finally, Hannah agrees with going back to him. After picking her up, the couple returns to home. She walks in to find pink and white flowers, arranged in the most delicate of vases. Her favorite chocolates scatter around the table and the gifts he laid out to surprise her, were a bonus to his heartfelt apology. Hannah embraces him while he wraps his arms around her, squeezing so gently, yet so firm. They both sigh of relief as though they had not seen one another for an extended period. Hannah surely forgives him, just as he had hoped.

Over the following months, things for once seemed to look much better, for them. He was home more often, and the two of them spent quality time together. They were at last, back where they started when he swept Hannah off her feet. She sensed the near hope she had longed for. All Hannah ever really required was his time, love, and loyalty. There was but one other thing that could extend their happiness, a baby. They tried for another, and it wasn't long before she finds out she is pregnant again. The two of them were both excited and nervous all at the same time. Before Hannah realizes, a couple months had flown by. After a few doctors' appointments, everything seems normal. She can't help but wish for another boy, and would soon find out. It was about three months into her pregnancy and four weeks before having an ultrasound, to reveal the sex. Hannah is overwhelmed with excitement, but follows the doctor's strict instructions, taking it easy. She stresses as little as possible and does everything she knows, to prevent losing another baby. She feels the familiar flutters of the baby moving and smiles, yet this pregnancy is different; She wakes in the morning with sudden nausea and lies down at night with indigestion. Hannah craves food, she rarely eats. I suppose french fries dipped in vanilla ice cream, with a drizzle of chocolate isn't too unusual. Pickles, which she despises becomes similarly appetizing.

Her best efforts to have a healthy baby leads her to sadness, yet again. She wakes up one morning bleeding. Hannah knew right away, something wasn't right. They confirm her fears when she visits the ER. It wasn't nearly as heartbreaking as the first, assuming because Hannah wasn't as far along, but it left her wondering why this kept happening. The doctors explained that she probably should have allowed more time to heal in between pregnancies.

It appears Hannah is persistent about having another baby. Perhaps, it was the suffering and loss previously experienced. She will never completely heal but having another baby might fulfill the void that left her heartbroken and empty. Questions continue to follow her and the wonders will haunt Hannah, for many days to come. She often tries to imagine what her son would look like, what kind of personality might he have and the hardest one is her wondering, is he alone?

We all like to think there's a gate where someone awaits to take the hand of our passing loved ones, as they show them the beauty of heaven and afterlife; where sickness is no longer becoming, people stay young forever, and pain and suffering don't exist. She can only hope that someone is taking care of him in such a way she wanted to, but just as Hannah is unsure of the existence of God, similarly, she is of heaven, too. Perhaps, if she had a little more faith, these hauntings could turn into a peaceful knowing. To know her son was so special, he would stay pure for all of eternity, not to enter our corrupt world of sin. Maybe he had been chosen as one of the purest and most precious angels, in heaven. Hannah's wonders will appear in her dreams. She only hears, but a small voice "Mother I touch your tears whenever you cry, my invisible fingers will soothe you, just as yours soothed me, you will often think of me and cry, but remember, it was your laughter and love that built my temporary home, while our hearts beat as one, you gave me the courage to go on in my journey, and now I will do the same for you," Hannah wakes with a great deal of peace, yet she still yearns for just a coddle with her baby.

10 Culture Shock

Hannah appears to be stir crazy. She sits in the house day after day, looking at the same walls, and thinking about much of the recent events, in her life. She decides it's time to get out of the house and go back to work.

I am looking forward to taking my mind off everything. I have a friend that works at a local call center and she puts in a good word to the supervisor for me; She says he will call me any day now and I'll be back to work in no time. Meanwhile, my partner has dabbed in a few different businesses, while I maintain the paperwork, in the evenings. From time to time, he mentions his family leaving their country and coming to the United States. This includes his Mom, Step Dad, Sister, and Brother-in-Law. He seems to be excited about it, and as always, I support him. For them to come, it require us to sponsor them, which means they will live with us until they get on their feet and can live on their own.

We search and finally find a house. Five bedrooms, two-and-a-half baths, a family room, a huge dining room and a separate living room; this should be big enough for us all to live in comfortably. I prepare for their arrival; spending the next few weeks, unpacking our stuff, shopping and making sure the necessities are available to them. A nice, comfy, cozy bed with freshly washed linens will definitely welcome them. This will be my first time meeting them, and I must go above and beyond, to extend the welcome.

  Before I know it, we are picking them up from the Airport to bring them home. I am prepared for the language barrier since they spoke no English and I didn't speak much Farsi. Though, I figure we would get through it together. His mom and sister are the most beautiful people I have ever met. They greet me with the warmest hug, one could imagine. Although I don't understand exactly what they are saying, I hear the excitement in their tones. His mom cries of happiness after not having seen her firstborn son for ten years. The step-dad shakes his hand firmly and extends a hug. Before now, the only things I knew about their culture is what he told me, which was very little.

  Hannah was about to experience a culture shock in her own home. Although his family appeared very pleasant, his mom and sister immediately welcomed themselves to re-arranging her entire house without her consent or input; after having only stayed the first night. She would return from work the following day to a terrible, unfamiliar fragrance, nearly knocking the wind out of her. Not understanding what the smell was that lingered for hours, she would soon learn. Apparently, it was a ritual, for them to burn "Esfand" in the house. It is like other rituals that use sage, instead. It represents a casting out of evil spirits, better known as a purification ritual. Besides the horrible smell, Hannah realizes that her furniture was not where she left it. Finding a dish in the cabinet would be a guessing game. Hannah was not sure how to take it but, it offends her. She mentions it to her partner, in a private conversation, but he offers no explanation, nor a solution. This was only the start of an uncomfortable situation; where she must eventually choose whether to stand up for herself or just allow his family to take over her house.

Hannah's partner stays gone, for days at a time, working. She agrees to cut back her hours, taking them to different appointments they had. Despite her best efforts to help, she was continuously being judged. Hannah would hear them talk loudly amongst themselves, only to become utterly silent after she enters the room. Although it was baffling, she senses not being welcome to their conversation. Eventually, Hannah assumes that part of their culture requires the women to stay home and slave, keeping the house in perfect order and making sure there's hot food available for the husband when he returns from work. Cumin, turmeric, onions, and garlic replace all other smells, while their way of life vastly revolves around cooking. It appeared as though his mom and sister are highly submissive to their husbands. They nearly bow at their feet, to please them. Apparently, it's obscene for women to have tattoos. She notices them pointing and giggling at hers, while other times, they stare with disgusts. Recently, Hannah enjoyed inviting her family and friends over for dinner and socialization, but she has become so uncomfortable in her home, she no longer holds gatherings.

Despite the discomfort, Hannah still tries to make the best of it. From time to time, she offers to cook dinner, and in return, they criticize the food. They literally make faces, similar to a child that dislikes something. I suppose, her food was far off, what they were familiar with and Hannah understands its different, but a smack across the face taught her early on, to never complain about food placed on the table. Her parents would remind her of the many people, without. She eventually stops offering to cook. Then, it turns into complaints; she didn't contribute to the shared duties of the women in the house. Hannah finally realizes that she is fighting a losing battle and concludes, there was nothing she could ever do that would be good enough to please them. As a result, she stays in her room most of the time, which was the only place she would feel relaxed. Luckily, for her, they soon found jobs, got cars, and moved out. At long last, Hannah finds comfort again.

11 Unconditional Love

The place had grown too big for the couple. They wind up purchasing their first house in the small county where Hannah grew up. She recognizes a familiar homey feeling in the country; where the smell of recently cut grass, fills and revives the air. Green appears much brighter here than in the city. Trees cover the skyline instead of the tall bulky buildings. The night skies give the naked eye the biggest and brightest stars. Although your neighbors may be further away than those who were previously close to you, they turn out to be greater of friends. Nature replaces the loud music and the boisterous sounds you often hear in the city. Hannah indulges in it all.

  She soon discovers being pregnant again. They were both more scared than anything. Perhaps, they doubt she would make it full term and fear being heartbroken, once more. The further along Hannah gets, the more she grew to be excited. She wished for a boy, but at her four-month check-up and ultrasound, the doctor confirms it's a girl. Hannah was happy to have made it this far. Four months quickly turns into six, and suddenly eight. Before Hannah knew it, she was subsequently down to the last few weeks. They picked the perfect name that would resemble that of their first baby's. The doctor scheduled her for induction, and she was on the way, at last, to have the baby she longed for. After many hours of labor, Hannah meets her perfect newborn. I suppose thick dark hair, slightly tanned skin, long legs, and big brown eyes were genes, passed along by Hannah's partner; since she, herself, is pale, moderately short, with green eyes. The couple was finally complete after the struggles they had previously overcome.

  Hannah would spend most of the following days at home caring for their baby while her partner worked to provide for them. Things seemed to calm down for a while as they started this new chapter in their lives. Hannah would look at her baby and smile, with tears. She found herself in disbelief; finally succeeding in the one thing she wanted more than anything else, a healthy baby. With every smile and coo, Hannah discovers an unconditional love in a way she never thought possible; an unselfishness that develops from the moment a mother finds out she's pregnant. Hannah would often stare into her baby's big brown eyes, reassuring her, there was nothing more important in the world than she. You may have witnessed the love a mother has for her newborn baby, but imagine the pain after having lost one. The grief Hannah previously felt, transformed into a more profound love that would make her newborn baby that much more special.

Eventually, his mom comes back around and embraces being a first-time Grandmother. There were still barriers and criticism; only now, in the form of parenting; though they would work through it. It was the shared love of the baby that would eventually create a bond between the two. Occasionally, the Grandmother would relieve Hannah at night, keeping the baby, while she rested. Hannah identifies a tenderness in her; It appears, the Grandmother has a newly found love, similar to that of a mother's. In the next four years, Hannah will have two more babies, both being girls. The three of them are precisely two years apart, in age.

12 The bad only gets worse

Hannah eventually gets a job driving a school bus, hoping to regain her independence. As you may guess, her partner never really changes. She wants to believe he had, but things suddenly take a turn for the worse. The police respond to many domestic assault calls, and he gets by, with a slap on the wrist, only to continue his assaults. He strangles Hannah on one occasion, while their children watch, desperate to help their mom. Later, he runs Hannah, with them in the car, off the road at 55 miles per hour. Soon after, he bashes her head against a wall, nearly knocking her unconscious and sending her to the hospital. Sadly, the children saw it all.

  As you read, you must wonder why Hannah did not leave him. We may never know for sure, but they later discovered that she was dealing with a Narcissist, similarly, a mastermind of psychological manipulation. The physical abuse was only temporary, but the most damaging was the emotional suffering. This allowed him to gain control and power over Hannah. The Narcissists purpose is to gain complete control over their victim's self-esteem, feelings of self-worth and even their identity; in so much depth, there are no words to explain.

  He uses guilt, blame, and victimhood as manipulative devices, leaving her to believe she caused their problems. Narcissism leads its victims to become dependent on their abusers and begins from the moment they meet. The abuser preys' by, at first, creating this profound image of trustworthiness, portraying themselves to be superheroes, swooping in to save the day. Just as quickly as he sweeps, he will drop you from the highest level of gravity and pick you right back up again; just before you dive completely into the pits of hell. If not recognized early on, his sadism will eventually show its face, uncovering the mask of disguise, used to charm you. It is being determined, victims of Narcissism suffer major trauma, which affects their brain.

Unfortunately, it can take years, even decades to recover. Even then, it's very unlikely to ever fully erase the effects caused by this trauma.

Often, he accuses Hannah of cheating on him; this is merely an excuse to inflict further physical violence, for his own twisted gratification. She tries to escape but, when she does, he stalks her until she eventually feels like she has no choice and comes back. Hannah notices him showing up in different places where he should not be. He calls back to back all hours of the night, only to force himself in, raping her. He threatens to run away to his country with their kids.

Hannah's partner must have been the luckiest criminal to walk Earth. After being served with protective orders and violating them, along with spending a few nights in jail, it did not stop him. Hannah concluded that she may never escape him, not if she relied upon law enforcement. Out of desperation, she emails a letter to a National News Station. Hannah explains the circumstances and how her unalienable rights were being denied at the hands of Law Enforcement and a repeated Criminal Refuge. She never received a response, neither sure anyone ever read it. Hannah had enough of the abuse, and the trauma her kids faced. It was the realization alone, of them suffering, that would ignite a determination to escape him, yet again; but it wouldn't be long before the inevitable happens.

It was November 12, 2015, when the reality of the vicious cycle I lived, would show itself. This man that appears being sent to

---

rescue me, with all his flaws, held me hostage in my most sacred place, home. It started with what was just another ordinary day. I return home from doing my morning bus run and would soon head back out. As I prepare breakfast, I turn to find him standing there, with a devilish demeanor. In his hand, he holds a gun. I at once understood that this wouldn't end well.

Once Again, I was in shock, but even more so now, than ever. For a moment, the entire world stopped, while I processed what was happening. As he flashes the gun, he states that if I refuse to re-establish our relationship, he would kill me, then himself. His fist never seemed as measurably intimidating as the object he held. I knew with this and just a quick moving of his finger, my life could be over. There would be no, hoping it would not hurt as bad later, this time. If I say just one wrong thing to provoke him, it might be the last thing I ever say. Trying to get away from him, like I did before, didn't seem like the smartest thing to do, in this situation. Even, if it were, there was no way to turn my back to him, not for a second and not with the gun in his hand. As my thoughts raced, I conclude that there were no hopes of escaping. I found myself, on my knees, yet again, but this time my desperation overpowers my ability to question whether God existed.

After making poor choices, for so long and calling the police several times, only to end up here; I knew I could not rely on them or myself. It could only be God that might save me. If it would end this way, I had at least, hoped I would go to heaven.

"Lord please, forgive my sins and my lack of faith" I pleaded over and over again, as I tried to prepare myself to die.

The sliding images in my head of the kid's faces, so sad and lonely because they would never see their mother again, were unbearable. My life wasn't in my hands, any longer. It was either in his hands or in the hands of God. During all the fights before, I never felt so powerless. There was an unfamiliar voice, telling me, remain calm, do not run, and don't fight. It left me paralyzed in fear.

Meanwhile, he freely waves the gun around and insists that I take him back. To end the confrontation, I agree, but that wasn't satisfying enough. For nearly an hour, of which felt like an eternity, we'd negotiate back and forth. At his mercy, I begged and pleaded for my life. "If you end our lives now, where does that leave them" I reminded him of our three girls that needed us more than anything. Although his actions, up to this point proved otherwise, I could only hope that, if nothing or no one else, he might have empathy for them. He still, rendered that if we were both dead, it wouldn't matter.

I suppose he was right. If it had ended that day, nothing would matter to either of us anymore. I would never tell them how much I loved them again. They would eventually get through it, just as everything else having been subjected to, in the hands of my horrible decisions and the monster, they called dad. They would never carry another burden of witnessing mama and daddy fight, again. Just maybe, they could eventually live a healthy life that every child deserves; free at last from the pain they suffered throughout their few years of life.

13 Faith Never Again Questioned

Despite his horrible intentions, God had other plans. He would leave the house with a warning; "if you call the cops, I will kill you next time" It was this expression, that signaled me to follow him, as he left. I knew, if they hadn't arrested him, I'd never have a peace of mind. While on the phone with the emergency operator and following him, I hope that by giving them his exact location, they would catch him. He must have gathered what I was doing, because he quickly got out of my sight. Not only did he get away from me, but the police too.

It wasn't until a couple months later, that he was arrested. Thanks to the due diligence of one, well-respected man, **Sheriff Joe McLaughlin Jr**. He must have exhausted all available resources to make sure justice was carried out. He may never know it, but will forever be my hero. I'm assuming he had help, but it was him alone that restored my faith in Law Enforcement and the principle of their existence. It went, without saying, but I believe something led me to his office crying and begging for help, for a greater reason than either of us may understand. I won't put words in his mouth, but I bet if you were to ask him; he might say, I was just doing my job; Digging into my most valid opinions, I say, he possesses a rare, profound dedication to protect and serve to the utmost of his capacity. He went well above, and beyond just doing his job. Mr. McLaughlin indirectly, reassured me I would soon regain peace in my life.

Before being arrested, Hannah's ex enjoys his freedom, while she remains a prisoner. It didn't seem fair, on any level of fairness. She was too afraid to go back to the house, but ran out of clothes for herself and the kids. Only with an escort, she returns home, to quickly gather some of their things. Hannah constantly looks over her shoulders. The fear of him popping up again seemed as if it would never make an exit. For months to come, the least little sound or hint of excitement triggered Hannah's thoughts "your life is in danger".

There is no way for Hannah to emphasize her most anxious feelings to anyone. She figures, the people closest to her can't relate, nor, will they understand. Hannah felt as though she was going crazy; before comprehending, her sensitivity is a normal reaction to the trauma. The only thing she knows to do, is control the outburst as much as possible and keep it hidden from everyone.

After him being arrested and locked up for six months, Hannah seems to be at ease. To her dismay, she only escapes him in a physical being. The trauma may never allow her to avoid him in thought, or while she sleeps. He is now again, a free man, while Hannah continues to wonder when he might show up, to finish what he started.

The dog barking at night signals, he is trying to get in the house. Hearing her kid's cry while they sleep, is a reminder, they too are troubled by their past. Entering a dark room triggers a profound weakness of incapacitation. Profiling strangers, while in a crowded public place, has become a measure of safety, for Hannah and her children. Trusting another man may never be possible, but so long as she keeps her guard up, she will never again become vulnerable, in such a way. The nightmares and illusions that haunt her, will eventually fade.

Above all else, Hannah's faith in God will never again be a questionable matter. If you think back, to every dangerous situation she found herself in, you will notice, it was a result from a decision or choice she made, prior. Besides, being overpowered by a Narcissist, she became her own worst enemy. Hannah thought she'd redeem their relationship, time and time again, convinced, it was for the sake of their kids. The only thing that ever needed to be redeemed, was her soul. For so long, she was oblivious to the fact, that it was for the same purpose of staying, that by doing so, would defeat itself. Remaining for the sake of the kids once meant, they wouldn't suffer a seperation.

Meanwhile, she overlooks them suffering the trauma and abuse they witnessed. Perhaps, if she surrenders to God, the way she did to the monster, Hannah might heal from it all. Either way, there is an undeniable fact that lies just beneath the surface of it all. It's only by the Grace of God and through discovering a Divine Strength, that she is here today, not nearly as broken, but stronger than ever, sharing her story. Hannah will go on, continuing to repair the brokenness of herself and the three beautiful girls that call her mom. She will also, set out to fulfill, what may have very well been her purpose all along, inspiring other women and children in similar circumstances.

The End

Inspiration from the Author

"Never Underestimate the Divine Strength of a Mother Who Appears Broken"

This phrase, in the most reciprocal form, is powerful. A broken woman is perceived as weak, battered, useless, and incapable, among many other low states of Human life, effortlessly causing her to think it might be best to lie down and die. The thought represents a desperation to escape a pain more powerful than she. There is, but one superseding power, greater than the pain itself. You take this woman, who loves her kids to the highest degree of unselfishness and give her a hint they're suffering. A Divine Strength that can't be seen, perhaps not even felt will ignite a fire within her from miles away. No one in its path will see it coming, not even her. This strength indicates that she will go beyond any limits to protect her offspring even if it means rising to her death. There's no mountain too high, no fire too crucible, nor a fear she won't face, to ensure they are safe, both mentally and physically. The best part is, no matter how broken down she appears, or how robbed she may be, no one can take from her, what they don't know she possesses. Following the exhaustion of all other choices, this strength is activated, only when it's most necessary. It may never be discovered in a lifetime by many, but you can bet it's there when you need it most. It's in every one of us, festering, waiting for what may be the last moments of life or death.

www.ingramcontent.com/pod-product-compliance
Lightning Source LLC
Chambersburg PA
CBHW040239240726
48664CB00001B/189